USING MATHS
BE A STUNTMAN

by
Wendy Clemson,
David Clemson and
Joss Gower

SKYDIVE
ARIZONA

USING
MATHS
BE A STUNTMAN

Copyright © ticktock Entertainment Ltd 2004

First published in Great Britain in 2004 by ticktock Media Ltd.,
Unit 2, Orchard Business Centre, North Farm Road, Tunbridge Wells, Kent, TN2 3XF

ISBN 1 86007 546 0 pbk
ISBN 1 86007 552 5 hbk
Printed in China

With thanks to our consultants: Steve Truglia (stuntman and stunt co-ordinator), Jenni Back and
Liz Pumfrey from the NRICH Project, Cambridge University and Debra Voege.
For their help with photographs, thanks goes to: Steve Truglia, Joe Jennings, Peter Hassall
and Paul Bickers. **Illustrations by** Stewart Johnson.

WENDY CLEMSON

Wendy is experienced in working with and for children, and has been writing full-time since 1989. Her publications, which now exceed one hundred, have been written for children and sometimes their parents and teachers. In her many maths books, the aim is always to present the reader with challenges that are fun to do.

DAVID CLEMSON

David has wide-ranging experience as a writer and educationalist. His publications list is prodigious. In collaboration with Wendy, David has worked on many maths books for children. He is fascinated by maths and logic puzzles and is keen for the reader to enjoy them too.

JOSS GOWER

Joss is an experienced action stunt double, performer and stunt co-ordinator. He appears regularly on TV and in movies performing the types of stunts featured in this book. His long list of TV and movie credits includes: *Harry Potter*, *Star Wars*, *Gladiator* and *The Mummy*. You can see Joss's full résumé at www.stunt-unit.com.

CONTENTS

NUMERACY WORK COVERED IN THIS BOOK:

Throughout this book there are opportunities to practise **addition, subtraction, multiplication** and **division** using both mental calculation strategies and pencil and paper methods.

CALCULATIONS:
- x2, x3, x10 TABLES: pg. 7
- x6, x7, x8, x9 TABLES: pgs. 11, 25

NUMBERS AND THE NUMBER SYSTEM:
- DECIMALS: pg. 10
- ESTIMATING (using a number line): pg. 24
- NUMBER SEQUENCES: pg. 27
- PLACE VALUE: pgs. 10, 17

SOLVING 'REAL LIFE' PROBLEMS:
- MEASURES: pg. 16
- MONEY: pg. 22
- TIME: pgs. 6, 10, 16

HANDLING DATA:
- USING TABLES/CHARTS/DIAGRAMS: pgs. 6, 8, 9, 12, 13, 15, 18, 20, 21, 22, 24, 25

MEASURES:
- AREA: pg. 9
- ESTIMATING: pg. 23
- ESTIMATING/CHECKING (times using seconds): pgs. 11, 23
- RELATIONSHIPS BETWEEN UNITS OF MEASUREMENT: pg. 15
- SCALES (estimating/reading from a scale): pg. 24
- TIME (reading from analogue clocks): pg. 6
- USING METRIC/IMPERIAL MEASUREMENTS: pgs. 9, 13, 15, 16, 20, 21, 23

SHAPE AND SPACE:
- 3-D SHAPES: pg. 26
- ANGLES: pg. 12
- COMPASS DIRECTIONS: pg. 18
- GRID CO-ORDINATES: pg. 18
- LINE SYMMETRY: pg. 11

HOW TO USE THIS BOOK

Maths is important in the lives of people everywhere. We use maths when we play a game, ride a bike, go shopping – in fact, all the time! Everyone needs to use maths at work. You may not realise it, but stuntmen and stuntwomen use maths when they are performing dramatic movie stunts. With this book you will get the chance to try lots of exciting maths activities using real life data and facts about stunt work. Practise your maths and numeracy skills and experience the thrill of what it's really like to be a professional stunt artist.

This exciting maths book is very easy to use – check out what's inside!

Fun to read information about the work of stuntmen and stuntwomen.

MONEY MATTERS

Today, the *car bail-out* (the jump from the car) is being filmed. A hidden stunt driver is driving the car along the pier at about 15 mph. The car has been specially modified so that there is room in the front for the driver and the two stunt doubles. At exactly the right moment, the stuntman and stuntwoman dive from the car and land on crash mats that have been placed along the car's route. When the film is **edited**, these shots of the jump will be blended with close-ups of the lead actors' faces and film of the car hitting the boat. With clever editing, it will look as if the two stars really jumped from their car as it crashed through the end of the pier.

MATHS ACTIVITIES

Look for the **STUNT WORK FILE**. You will find real life maths activities and questions to try.

To answer some of the questions, you will need to collect data from a DATA BOX. Sometimes, you will need to collect facts and data from the text or from charts and diagrams.

Be prepared! You will need a pen or pencil and a notebook for your workings and answers.

STUNT WORK FILE

One important aspect of a stunt co-ordinator's work is to make sure that the stunt can be performed within the **budget**. After a long day working on the **set**, you still have some paperwork to do!

In the DATA BOX you will see the budget for the *"Countdown"* stunt. Use the information to make these cost calculations:

1) What is the total cost of the stunt doubles for the lead actor and actress if they are working on set for two days?
2) How much will the two divers cost if it takes them four days to recover the wreckage?
3) How much more does the speedboat for the shoot cost than the test boat?
4) How much more does a stunt double earn than the stunt driver, if they both work for two days?
5) If all the work takes two days, how much will the total costs be?
   (Remember to include all the vehicles, the stunt performers and the crew.)
   (You will find a TIP to help you with these questions on page 29)

TRICKS OF THE TRADE

Cars used in stunts can be rigged so that it is possible to drive them from the passenger side or even from behind the driver's seat. Sometimes the real driver's seat is taken out and replaced with a smaller one. A hidden stunt driver then sits on the small seat covered in a fabric that matches the car's upholstery – the driver is actually camouflaged as a car seat!

STUNT WORK FACTS

The car door and the area around the door are checked for anything that might catch on the stunt performers' clothes as they dive away from the car. The stuntman and stuntwoman wear protective padding under their costumes. Sometimes stunt performers even wear thin helmets hidden under a wig.

22

Fun to read stunt work facts.

DATA BOX

If you see one of these boxes, there will be important data inside that will help you with the maths activities.

MATHS ACTIVITIES

Feeling confident? Try these extra **CHALLENGE QUESTIONS.**

The stuntwoman dives from the car.

In the movie, the lead actor will drive a real Ferrari costing hundreds of thousands of pounds. For the stunt work, a much cheaper 'kit car' (replica) will be used.

DATA BOX — STUNT BUDGET

Stunt driver (*to drive the car and truck*)	£500 per day
Stuntman double for the lead actor	£750 per day
Stuntwoman double for the lead actress	£750 per day
Two divers (*to recover car and boat wreckage*)	£400 per day each
Five safety marshals	£100 per day each
Truck for towing the car and boat (*hire cost*)	£250 per day
Speedboat for shoot	£10 000
Ferrari *kit car* for shoot	£15 000
Test boat for practising the stunt	£2000
Test car for practising the stunt	£2000

CHALLENGE QUESTIONS

Before they can prepare a detailed plan, a stunt co-ordinator must be able to make an **estimate** of what will happen in a stunt.

Use your powers of estimation to choose which of these measurements is closest to an actual happening.

a) A speeding stunt car is travelling at:
50 mph   500 mph   5 mph

b) When a driver presses on the brake pedal, a car starts to brake after:
4 minutes   ¼ second   40 seconds

c) The length of a stuntman's arm is:
15 cm   50 cm   85 cm   15 m

23

IF YOU NEED HELP...

TIPS FOR MATHS SUCCESS

On pages 28 – 29 you will find lots of tips to help you with your maths work.

ANSWERS

Turn to pages 30 – 31 to check your answers. (Try all the activities and questions before you take a look at the answers.)

GLOSSARY

On page 32 there is a glossary of stunt and movie words and a glossary of maths words. The glossary words appear **in bold** in the text.

A CAREER IN THE MOVIES

Stuntmen and stuntwomen lead busy and exciting lives. During a day's work, they might be asked to smash up an expensive car, jump off a building, ride a motorbike off a cliff or leap from a plane! They travel to exciting locations all over the world and get the chance to work alongside famous movie and TV stars. Stuntmen and stuntwomen see their names in the credits of major film and television productions, and they sometimes receive fan mail – just like the actors and actresses that they *double* (take the place of). Stunt performers can be asked to play a wide variety of characters – police officers, doctors, astronauts, aliens, Jedi Knights and gladiators!

STUNT WORK FILE

When working on a movie, stunt performers advise the actors and the director on the safest way to perform and film dangerous stunts. They also work with the **special effects** people to set up explosions and sometimes even help to design the movie **sets**.

Use the clocks in the DATA BOX to answer these questions about a stuntman's action-packed day.

1) What is the stuntman doing at these times of day: *10:55 am, 6:35 am, 5:15 pm* and *7:47 pm*?
2) In total, how much time does the stuntman spend rehearsing the sword fight?
3) For how long is the stuntman on set after lunch?
4) How long was the stuntman's meeting with the director?

(You will find a TIP to help you with questions 2 and 3 on page 28)

Stuntman, Steve Truglia rehearses a gladiator sword fight.

STUNT WORK FACT

Stunt performers have to keep fit. They take part in sports that are good for all-round fitness, such as running and swimming, and sports that involve lots of stretching, such as gymnastics and yoga. Being strong and fit gives you confidence when you are performing a difficult stunt move.

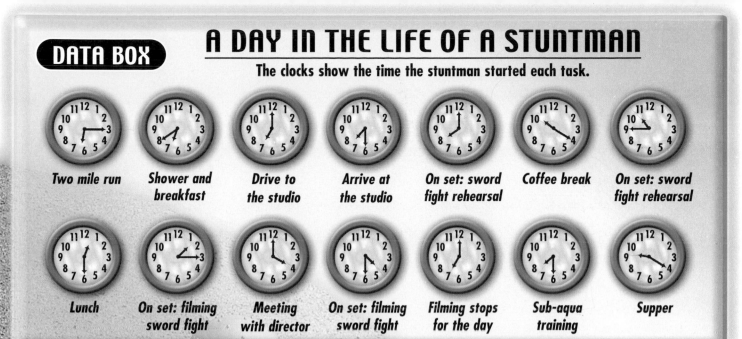

A DAY IN THE LIFE OF A STUNTMAN

DATA BOX

The clocks show the time the stuntman started each task.

Two mile run	Shower and breakfast	Drive to the studio	Arrive at the studio	On set: sword fight rehearsal	Coffee break	On set: sword fight rehearsal

Lunch	On set: filming sword fight	Meeting with director	On set: filming sword fight	Filming stops for the day	Sub-aqua training	Supper

Some stunt performers learn martial arts, such as judo and kickboxing.

A stuntwoman learns how to fly through the air on a high trapeze!

STUNT SKILLS FACT

Stunt performers learn specialist skills to use in their work, such as skydiving, wire-walking, abseiling, rock climbing, sword fighting and bareback horse riding. They even learn how to fall downstairs without hurting themselves!

CHALLENGE QUESTIONS

In every week, a stuntwoman spends 14 hours training for all the specialist skills she uses in her job.

Complete these statements:
a) In every 2 weeks, the stuntwoman spends ? hours training.
b) In every 3 weeks, the stuntwoman spends ? hours training.
c) In every 10 weeks, the stuntwoman spends ? hours training.

PERFORMING HIGH FALLS

A screaming woman is falling from the roof of a building. She waves her arms and somersaults as she plummets towards the ground, 25 metres below. But this is not a terrible accident – the woman is a stunt performer, and she is filming a dramatic *high fall* for a movie. Every second of her fall has been carefully planned, rehearsed and tested. As the director shouts, *"Cut"*, the stuntwoman makes a perfect landing in the middle of a huge airbag. Stuntmen and stuntwomen learn how to fall and how to land. If a stunt performer does not land in the right position, they can badly injure themselves. If they miss their **landing rig**, a fall could be fatal.

STUNT WORK FILE

A stuntman is performing some high falls for a movie. The movie **set** is an old warehouse building.

In the DATA BOX, you will see a plan of the movie set (as it would look if viewed from above). You are helping the stuntman to set up the landing rigs in the right place for each fall.
(For example, if the stuntman jumps from the roof at square D8, he will need an airbag in square D7.)

In which square should an airbag be placed, if the stuntman jumps:
1) From the roof, between the balcony and the fire escape?
2) From the top of the fire escape to the ground below?

In which squares should airbags be placed, if the stuntman jumps:
3) From the window ledge across to the parapet?
4) From anywhere on the balcony?
5) From anywhere on the parapet?

A stuntman practises a high fall onto an airbag.

STUNT WORK FACT

Most actors and actresses do not perform their own stunts, because if they suffer an injury, they will not be able to act in the rest of the movie or TV show. Specially trained stuntmen and stuntwomen take their place, performing in any scenes that are dangerous or require specialist skills.

TRICKS OF THE TRADE

A *safety spotter*, normally another stunt person, will keep watch from out of **shot** during a stunt. If a stunt performer gets into trouble, the spotter will be ready to help. For example, repositioning a crash mat at the last moment, if a stuntman has made a jump and it looks as though he might land in the wrong place!

PLAN OF THE MOVIE SET

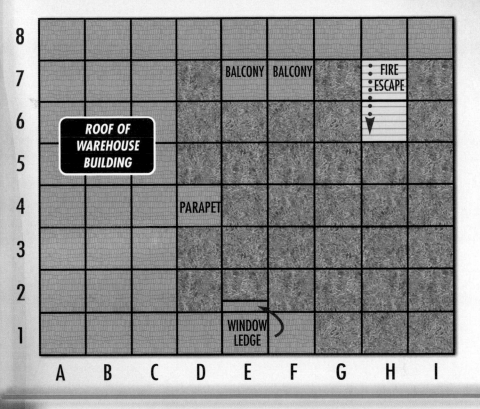

	A	B	C	D	E	F	G	H	I
8									
7					BALCONY	BALCONY		FIRE ESCAPE	
6	ROOF OF								
5	WAREHOUSE BUILDING								
4				PARAPET					
3									
2					WINDOW				
1					LEDGE				

The airbag is deflated and carefully rolled up by the crew.

CHALLENGE QUESTIONS

Stunt performers use different sized airbags for different heights of fall.

a) Stunt performers must be able to work out if the airbag they want to use will fit on a movie set. Work out the **area** of each of these airbags.

Height of fall	AIRBAG DIMENSIONS		
	Length (ft)	Width (ft)	Height (ft)
30 ft	12	8	4
50 ft	14	12	6
70 ft	15	14	8
100 ft	25	20	10
150 ft	30	25	15

b) You can work out how much air there is in an airbag by multiplying *the length by the width by the height*.

The answer will be in *cubic feet*. How many cubic feet of air will be in the airbag used for a fall of 100 feet?

(You will find TIPS to help you with these questions on page 28)

PERFORMING FIRE BURNS

When you watch a movie villain burst into flames, it's easy to forget that there's actually a real person under all the fire and smoke. Fire burns are only ever carried out by experienced stunt performers. A safety team of firemen, crew members with fire extinguishers and paramedics will be on the **set**, and a timekeeper will time the stunt to make sure that the fire is put out at exactly the right moment. When performing full body fire burns, stuntmen and stuntwomen are completely covered in special fireproof clothing. They also hold their breath in case they breathe in the flames – this could seriously injure or even kill them.

STUNT WORK FILE

Today, you are the timekeeper in a fire burn stunt. The stuntman will be on fire for 20 seconds and must carry out the following actions:

- Open a door.
- Fall forward.
- Roll over.
- Get up, then fall again.
  (The safety crew will then put out the fire.)

You must check that everything the stuntman needs to do, can be done within 20 seconds.

1) If it takes 3.2 seconds to open the door, how long is left for the stunt?

2) If the stuntman takes 4.8 seconds to fall forward and 8.5 seconds to roll over, how much time is left now?

3) Your watch says 11:07 and 55 seconds at the beginning of the stunt. What is the time when the fire burn is over?

(You will find a TIP to help you with question 3, on page 28)

A partial fire burn. The stuntman is wearing protective gel on his face and hair and four pairs of special, fireproof gloves.

STUNT WORK FACT

A special substance is used to create the flames for fire burns. This substance is pasted all over the stunt performer's fireproof clothes and then ignited. When a stuntman or stuntwoman is on fire, they must keep moving and ducking around the flames to avoid being burned.

TRICKS OF THE TRADE

When doing full body fire burns, stuntmen and stuntwomen wear fire suits made from fire-resistant materials, such as Nomex or Kevlar. They also wear masks made from a special silicon mixture, with heat-resistant glass in the eye holes to protect their eyes. A special antiseptic gel, that has been cooled in the fridge, is spread on any exposed areas of skin. The gel helps to keep the stunt performer's skin cool, as the fire heats up, and, if the stunt performer is burned, the antiseptic works on their skin straight away. Sometimes stunt performers soak their heat-resistant underwear in the gel overnight – in the fridge!

During this full body fire burn, the temperature of the fire was about 800°C.

CHALLENGE QUESTIONS

During a 20 second fire burn, a stunt performer is under a lot of pressure. They must hold their breath, act out their role and avoid being burned.

See how well you can concentrate under pressure by timing yourself doing these tasks. Which can you do in 20 seconds?

a) Count in 5s to 500 (starting at zero).

b) Say the six times table backwards, starting with *'ten times six is sixty'*.

c) Write the word STUNTMAN; decide which letters show line symmetry, then mark in the **lines of symmetry**.

BE A STUNT DRIVER

An action movie would be a big disappointment if it did not include at least one car chase or dramatic crash! Stunt drivers learn how to manoeuvre vehicles at high speed, without risking injury to themselves, other actors or crew members. They also learn how to position or stop their vehicle on an exact spot, called a *mark*. Movie and TV **plots** require stunt drivers to drive vehicles off buildings, crash into other vehicles, drive on just two wheels and miss things with only centimetres to spare. Stunt drivers also learn how to perform exciting high speed moves, such as skids, spins and handbrake turns!

STUNT WORK FILE

If a stunt driver misses their *mark*, they could crash into a camera, a piece of the **set** or even a person!

A stunt driver is asked to make four manoeuvres. She must drive in a straight line then slide the car **clockwise** and stop in the positions shown below.

1) Through what **angle** has the car turned in each of the manoeuvres?

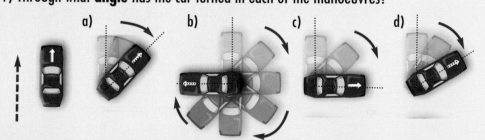

Next the stunt driver reverses at high speed. She uses the handbrake and the steering wheel to make the car slide around. Then she puts the car into first gear and speeds off, all the time travelling in the same direction without stopping or slowing down!

2) Through how many **degrees** does the car turn in this manoeuvre?

3) Now look at this skid. How many degrees has the car turned through here?

(You will find TIPS to help you with these questions on page 28)

DATA BOX
STOPPING DISTANCES

SPEED (mph)	STOPPING DISTANCE (Number of car lengths)
20	3
30	6
40	9
50	13
60	18
70	24

A stunt driver and stuntman perform a 'car knock-down' stunt.

CHALLENGE QUESTIONS

A stunt driver is asked to stop from high speed in front of a stuntwoman. This is how he would plan and test the stunt.

Drive along at the right speed then slam on the brakes. Measure how long it takes to slide to a stop. Use this *stopping distance measurement* to work out where the stuntwoman will stand, and how far from the stuntwoman to apply the brakes.

Practise the stop several times, to make sure the stopping distance is the same each time.

Use the information in the DATA BOX to answer these questions about measuring stopping distances:

a) If a stunt car is 3 metres long and is being driven at 50 mph, what is the stopping distance in metres?

b) A stunt car travelling at 30 mph takes 27 metres to stop. How long is the car?

c) A car is 4 metres long. What speed is it travelling at, if the driver takes 96 metres to stop?

TRICKS OF THE TRADE

When stopping on a *mark*, especially in front of a person, a wire rope will often be attached to the rear of the car, and then attached to a fixed object, such as a tree or truck. This safety measure ensures the person is not hit if the car accidentally overruns its stopping *mark*!

BE A STUNT CO-ORDINATOR

Stunt co-ordinators are the experts who design and arrange stunts. They are generally ex-stuntmen or stuntwomen who have lots of experience. Stunt co-ordinators work with **special effects** people, **set** and costume designers and even the make-up artists, so they have to understand what all the different departments in a film unit do. Stunt co-ordinators find the right stuntman or stuntwoman for a job, they arrange the stunt to a **budget** and they rehearse the stunt with the performers. When planning or filming a stunt, the co-ordinator is responsible for the safety of all the performers and crew on the set.

STUNT WORK FILE

On the car chase map you will see five possible routes that a stunt co-ordinator is considering for a car chase.

Follow each of the car chase routes. As you pass through a calculation work out the missing number.

Then sum the missing numbers for each route.

(You will find TIPS to help you with these calculations on page 28)

STUNT WORK FACT

The audience must never see that a stunt double has taken the place of an actor. In a car chase, a stunt driver does the driving, but the actor is filmed in close-up sitting in the car. The stunt co-ordinator makes sure that both performers' movements and positions are exactly the same. In the final film, it will be impossible to tell that two different people played the car driver.

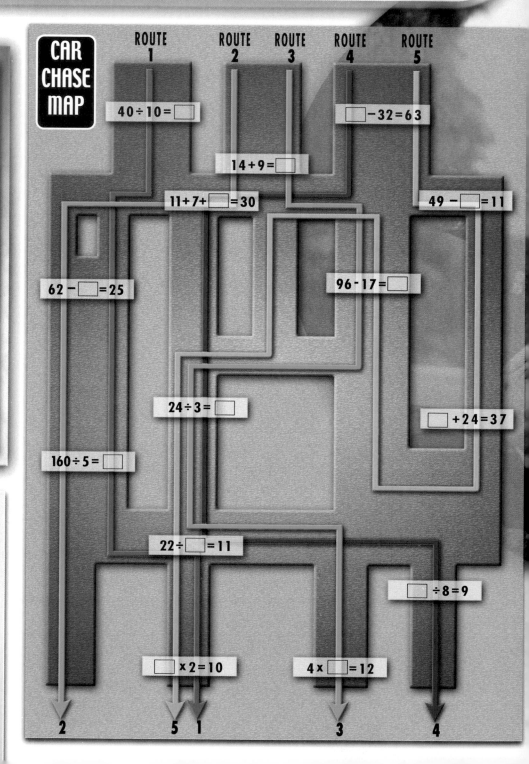

CAR CHASE MAP

ROUTE 1 ROUTE 2 ROUTE 3 ROUTE 4 ROUTE 5

$40 \div 10 = \square$

$\square - 32 = 63$

$14 + 9 = \square$

$11 + 7 + \square = 30$

$49 - \square = 11$

$62 - \square = 25$

$96 - 17 = \square$

$24 \div 3 = \square$

$\square + 24 = 37$

$160 \div 5 = \square$

$22 \div \square = 11$

$\square \div 8 = 9$

$\square \times 2 = 10$

$4 \times \square = 12$

2   5 1   3   4

MOTORCYCLE STUNTS

Motorcycle stunt riders appear in movies and TV shows. Many top riders also *WOW* audiences at special live shows by attempting record-breaking, long-distance jumps.

THE STUNTMAN	THE STUNT	LENGTH OF JUMP
Jason Rennie	Made a MONSTER ramp-to-ramp jump on 9th July, 2000.	77 metres 11 cm
Doug Danger	Jumped an L-1011 jumbo jet, wing tip to wing tip.	48 768 millimetres
Johnny Airtime	Jumped a moving train head on — the train actually went under him!	54.86 metres
Doug Danger	Jumped 42 cars.	76 500 millimetres
Kaptain Robbie Knievel	Jumped a 762-metre-deep gorge at the Grand Canyon.	6949 centimetres
Johnny Airtime	Jumped from a ramp to land on a moving truck.	41 m 15 cm

A car chase ends with a car crashing into a delivery truck!

A high speed tracking vehicle used for filming car chases. It can carry camera operators and their equipment.

CHALLENGE QUESTIONS

Stunt motorcycle riders use take-off and landing ramps, and sometimes they build **landing rigs** of huge piles of cardboard boxes!

Use the DATA BOX information to answer these questions:

a) How long was Doug Danger's jumbo jet jump, in metres?

b) Which of the jumps is the longest?

(You will find information about UNITS OF MEASUREMENT on page 29)

PERFORMING AERIAL STUNTS

Sometimes movie **plots** or ideas for TV commercials require the action to take place thousands of feet above the ground. Specialist skydiving stunt co-ordinators plan and carry out dramatic, and sometimes bizarre, aerial stunts. Stunt skydivers can be asked to jump from planes, helicopters or tall cliffs. They are accompanied by specially trained camera operators who record the action using cameras mounted on their helmets. The stunt performers act out their roles, according to the **script**, while the cameraman captures their manoeuvres on film. All this, while **freefalling** towards the earth at around 120 mph!

STUNT WORK FILE

Today you are joining a team filming an aerial stunt for a pizza delivery commercial. When you jump from the plane, you and your cameraman will have just over a minute of freefall time to get the required **shots** before you need to open your parachutes.

As you exit the plane, you are at an altitude of 16 000 feet AGL (Above Ground Level).

You will be freefalling at approximately 1000 feet every 5 seconds.

1) How far do you freefall in one second?
2) How far do you freefall in ten seconds?
3) At an altitude of 2500 feet, you open your parachute. How far did you fall in freefall?
4) After how many seconds of freefall do you open your parachute?

Aerial cinematographer, Joe Jennings at work.

SKYDIVING FACT

Skydivers use altimeters to show them how far they have dropped. These special gauges look a bit like a clock face. A needle moves around the face showing the skydiver his altitude (height above the ground). When he reaches 2500 ft (762 m) the skydiver must open his parachute. At this height, the skydiver has just 12 seconds left before he hits the ground.

A skydiving team go for a drive at 12 500 feet.

The team have a softer landing than their car!

A skydiver with an important delivery!

CHALLENGE QUESTIONS

A stunt skydiving team are planning to jump a car out of a plane! Here is some information about the stunt:

- Weight of the car and four skydivers: 1230 kilograms.
- Exit altitude: 12 500 feet AGL (Above Ground Level).
- Time to impact: approximately 70 seconds.
- Time in freefall (riding in the car): 40 seconds.
- Skydivers will exit the car: at 4500 feet.
- Time to impact as jumpers leave car: approximately 20 seconds.

When skydiving, it is essential you read measurements and timings accurately. Use the figures in the *car jump stunt* to check what you know about *place value*.

a) What does the '4' in 4500 represent?
b) What does the '4' in 40 represent?
c) What does the '2' in 1230 represent?
d) What does the '1' in 12 500 represent?

(You will find information about PLACE VALUE on page 28)

PLANNING A MOVIE STUNT

A top movie director wants you to arrange a nail-biting final sequence for a new action movie called *"Countdown"*. A villain is speeding towards a crowded beach in a speedboat packed with explosives. The movie's two heroes will stop the speedboat by driving their car off the end of a pier and crashing it into the boat. The stunt will make a truly explosive end to the movie – all you have to do is figure out how to make it happen! It is easy to get a car to hit a stationary target, but the boat will be moving at high speed. There will be a stuntman and a stuntwoman in the car and a driver on the boat – how do we prevent them from being injured?

STUNT WORK FILE

You have devised a brilliant way to perform the *"Countdown"* stunt!

A truck will tow both the car and boat using a clever system of pulleys and wires attached to the vehicles. When the truck moves forward, the car and boat will move together at the same speed – on a collision course! As the car reaches the end of the pier, its wire will be released. The car will keep moving off the end of the pier and hit the boat. There will be no need to have anyone in the car or boat!

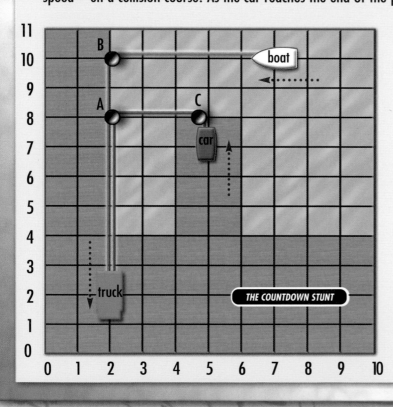

THE COUNTDOWN STUNT

The diagram shows how the car and boat will be pulled together.

1) What is the length in whole squares from the truck to pulley A?

2) What is the total length in whole squares of the cable that joins the boat and truck?

3) What are the co-ordinates of the following:
   • The boat   • Pulley wheel B   • The truck

4) What is found at point (2,8) on the grid?

5) What do you think the co-ordinates will be of the point where the car and boat will crash?

(You will find TIPS to help you with questions 3, 4 and 5 on page 29)

CHALLENGE QUESTIONS
Using the diagram and compass, answer the following questions:

a) Which vehicle is south-east of pulley B?   b) Which vehicle is south-west of pulley C?

The "Countdown" stunt has been storyboarded (sketched by a special artist). Everyone involved in planning the stunt can now see what will happen.

1 The car speeds towards the pier.

2 The boat will pass by the end of the pier in a fraction of a second.

3

CAR

BOAT

CAR

The two heroes leap from the car.

PAN WITH BOAT

The jump from the car will actually be filmed as a separate stunt. It will then be carefully **edited** (joined together) with film of the crash.

A **special effects** team will blow up the boat by remote control as the car crashes into it.

4 The car smashes into the side of the speedboat causing a huge explosion.

FINDING A STUNTMAN FOR "COUNTDOWN"

Your idea for the *"Countdown"* stunt is a big success with the director. You will be the stunt co-ordinator for the movie, and must now begin work on the preparations for the stunt. **Shooting** begins soon! One of your main tasks will be to find a stuntman and a stuntwoman to double the two lead characters. All stunt performers have a *résumé*. This document contains details of their stunt skills, their past work and all their physical characteristics. Movie and TV directors, casting agents and stunt co-ordinators use these *résumés* when choosing a stunt performer to double for a particular actor or actress, or when they need a stunt person with a special skill.

STUNT WORK FILE

In the DATA BOX you will see the *résumés* for five stuntmen.

1) Which stuntman can rock climb and has brown hair?

2) Which stuntman is taller than 185 cm, cannot street fight, but can skydive?

3) Who would not be suitable to double for an actor over 185 cm in height?

4) Who would you choose to double in a fire burn stunt for an actor who is 180 cm tall and weighs 102 kg?

In the DATA BOX there are descriptions of the stunt skills needed for three projects.

5) Which stuntmen have the right skills for:
- The TV commercial
- The hospital drama
- The *"Countdown"* movie

(You will find a TIP to help you with these questions on page 29)

Résumés contain details of a stunt performer's physical characteristics.

Hair colour

Eye colour

Height

Weight and build

Shoe size

TRICKS OF THE TRADE

Sometimes stuntmen and stuntwomen will dye their hair, or wear wigs and disguises or extra padding to make them look more like the actor or actress they are doubling.

DATA BOX STUNTMEN RESUMES

STUNTMAN	ALEC	PAUL	DAVID	CHRIS	ED
Height (cm):	178	195	178	187	180
Weight (kg):	79	98	105	102	90
Shoe size:	9	11	9	10	9
Hair colour:	Blond	Brown	Brown	Black	Brown
Eye colour:	Brown	Brown	Brown	Blue	Brown
STUNT SKILLS	Fire burn	Car bail-out	Fire burn	Bareback horse riding	Bungee jumping
	Car bail-out	Car knock-down	Sword fighting	Saddle falls	Skateboarding
	Street fighting	Stair fall	Car knock-down	Skydiving	Skydiving
	Rock climbing	Skydiving	Street fighting	Cowboy fighting	Car bail-out
	Skateboarding	Rock climbing	Car bail-out	Street fighting	Trapeze

STUNT	"COUNTDOWN" MOVIE	HOSPITAL DRAMA	TV COMMERCIAL
STUNT SKILLS NEEDED	Fire burn	Car knock-down	Skydiving
	Car bail-out	Stair fall	Trapeze
	Street fighting	Rock climbing	Skateboarding

A stuntman and stuntwoman learn how to fight.

Facial features are important. Stunt performers need to look like the actor or actress they are doubling.

CHALLENGE QUESTION

The lead actor in the "Countdown" movie is 178 centimetres tall, weighs 79 kilograms and has brown hair and brown eyes.

Which of the stuntmen will be the best double for this actor?

21

Today, the *car bail-out* (the jump from the car) is being filmed. A hidden stunt driver is driving the car along the pier at about 15 mph. The car has been specially modified so that there is room in the front for the driver and the two stunt doubles. At exactly the right moment, the stuntman and stuntwoman dive from the car and land on crash mats that have been placed along the car's route. When the film is **edited**, these shots of the jump will be blended with close-ups of the lead actors' faces and film of the car hitting the boat. With clever editing, it will look as if the two stars really jumped from their car as it crashed through the end of the pier.

STUNT WORK FILE

One important aspect of a stunt co-ordinator's work is to make sure that the stunt can be performed within the **budget**. After a long day working on the **set**, you still have some paperwork to do!

In the DATA BOX you will see the budget for the *"Countdown"* stunt.
Use the information to make these cost calculations:

1) What is the total cost of the stunt doubles for the lead actor and actress if they are working on set for two days?
2) How much will the two divers cost if it takes them four days to recover the wreckage?
3) How much more does the speedboat for the shoot cost than the test boat?
4) How much more does a stunt double earn than the stunt driver, if they both work for two days?
5) If all the work takes two days, how much will the total costs be?
   (Remember to include all the vehicles, the stunt performers and the crew.)

(You will find a TIP to help you with these questions on page 29)

TRICKS OF THE TRADE

Cars used in stunts can be rigged so that it is possible to drive them from the passenger side or even from behind the driver's seat. Sometimes the real driver's seat is taken out and replaced with a smaller one. A hidden stunt driver then sits on the small seat covered in a fabric that matches the car's upholstery – the driver is actually camouflaged as a car seat!

STUNT WORK FACTS

The car door and the area around the door are checked for anything that might catch on the stunt performers' clothes as they dive away from the car. The stuntman and stuntwoman wear protective padding under their costumes. Sometimes stunt performers even wear thin helmets hidden under a wig.

DATA BOX ▸ STUNT BUDGET

Stunt driver (*to drive the car and truck*)	£500	per day
Stuntman double for the lead actor	£750	per day
Stuntwoman double for the lead actress	£750	per day
Two divers (*to recover car and boat wreckage*)	£400	per day each
Five safety marshals	£100	per day each
Truck for towing the car and boat (*hire cost*)	£250	per day
Speedboat for shoot	£10 000	
Ferrari *kit car* for shoot	£15 000	
Test boat for practising the stunt	£2000	
Test car for practising the stunt	£2000	

The stuntwoman dives from the car.

In the movie, the lead actor will drive a real Ferrari costing hundreds of thousands of pounds. For the stunt work, a much cheaper 'kit car' (replica) will be used.

CHALLENGE QUESTIONS

Before they can prepare a detailed plan, a stunt co-ordinator must be able to make an **estimate** of what will happen in a stunt.

Use your powers of estimation to choose which of these measurements is closest to an actual happening.

a) A speeding stunt car is travelling at:
   50 mph   500 mph   5 mph

b) When a driver presses on the brake pedal, a car starts to brake after:
   4 minutes   ¼ second   40 seconds

c) The length of a stuntman's arm is:
   15 cm   50 cm   85 cm   15 m

ON SET: PREPARING FOR THE SHOOT

I t is early morning on the day of the crash shoot. The speedboat is anchored out in the harbour and the car is ready on the dock. The boat and car are attached by long wires to the tow bar of a huge truck. With the stunt rigged (set up), the camera crew are making their own final preparations. There are cameras mounted on tripods and on tracks running along the pier. A dramatic aerial shot of the crash will be filmed by a camera mounted on a huge crane. Out in the harbour, a cameraman on board a helicopter is ready to film the explosion. Every second of the *"Countdown"* stunt will be caught on film, from every possible position.

STUNT WORK FILE

The *grip* crew are the experts who set up and move the cameras.

One way to move a camera is to use a special trolley called a **dolly**. Sometimes tracks are used for moving cameras. The camera is mounted on a special type of dolly and the dolly is then moved up and down the track, a bit like a train.

1) Here is a section from the track on the pier. The places where the camera will be moved to are marked. **Estimate** how far along the track the camera is for each shot.

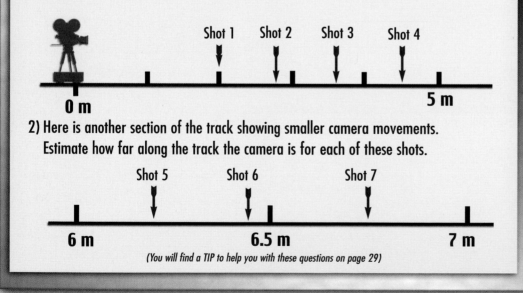

2) Here is another section of the track showing smaller camera movements. Estimate how far along the track the camera is for each of these shots.

(You will find a TIP to help you with these questions on page 29)

TRICKS OF THE TRADE

When filming actors inside a moving car, cameras can be mounted on the bonnet of the vehicle to film through the windscreen. Cameras can also be mounted on *hostess trays* — named after the trays used in drive-in burger restaurants in the USA. The camera is positioned on the side of the car (just like a *hostess tray*) and the action is filmed through the driver or passenger's window.

TRICKS OF THE TRADE

When filming a moving vehicle, the *picture car* (the vehicle being filmed) can be mounted on a low trailer and towed along. The position of the picture car still looks natural in relation to the road and the actors do not need to perform and drive at the same time.

A London taxi cab is towed by a special low-loader. The camera operators can film from in here.

CHALLENGE QUESTIONS

When working on a movie, lots of time is spent waiting for other crew members to do their work.

While the grip crew set up the cameras, take a break and see if you can find the missing numbers in these *number cross* clues.

(For example, the answer to "1 across" is 48, so the clue is 6 x 8.)

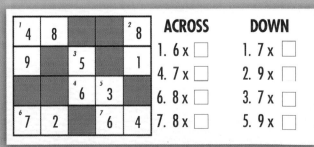

¹4	8			²8
9		³5		1
		⁴6	⁵3	
⁶7	2		⁷6	4

ACROSS
1. 6 x ☐
4. 7 x ☐
6. 8 x ☐
7. 8 x ☐

DOWN
1. 7 x ☐
2. 9 x ☐
3. 7 x ☐
5. 9 x ☐

ON SET: THE SHOOT

The cameras are in place and the **special effects** team have set up the explosion. Everyone is ready to film the crash sequence – it is time to go for a *take*. The director shouts, *"Action"* and the truck starts to pull the boat and car. The vehicles get faster and faster. When the car reaches the end of the pier, its wire is released. The car soars through the air towards the boat. As the two vehicles impact, a special effects **pyrotechnician** sets off the explosion by remote control. Flames, smoke, bits of car and pieces of boat fly up into the sky. The director shouts, *"Cut"*. There are claps and cheers from the crew. The stunt has worked perfectly – *it's a wrap!*

STUNT WORK FILE

The stunt team's work is finished.
Now the divers can begin recovering the wreckage
of the boat and car.

Here are some pieces of debris recovered from the harbour
after the explosion. Look at these **3-D (three dimensional)**
shapes carefully and then answer the questions.

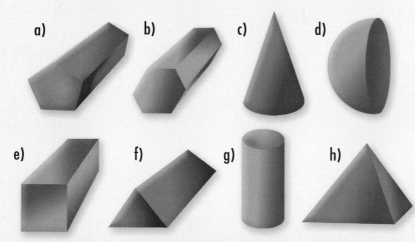

a)   b)   c)   d)

e)   f)   g)   h)

1) The cone (c) has an **apex**. Which other shape has an apex?
2) Which shapes have at least one circular **face**?
3) Which shapes are **prisms**?
4) How many straight **edges** do each of the prisms have?
5) What can you say about the number of edges each time?

STUNT WORK FACT

The area around a stunt shoot is *locked off* (closed off) by the safety marshals. This prevents any members of the public wandering onto the part of the **set** where a stunt is being filmed.

SPECIAL EFFECTS FACT

When filming an explosion, you normally only have one chance to get it right. The special effects team have put an explosive device on board the speedboat. When it is detonated, the explosive charge will break up the body of the boat. The pyrotechnicians have also put petrol and a special black powder inside the boat to create a dramatic, highly visual explosion.

CHALLENGE QUESTIONS

In order for a stunt to be successful, the sequence of events has to be worked out carefully.

Try working out these number sequences to see how good you are at putting things in the right order.

What are the next three numbers in each sequence?
a) 12, 19, 26, 33, _ , _ , _
b) 101, 104, 107, 110, _ , _ , _
c) 32, 29, 26, 23, _ , _ , _

What are the missing numbers in these sequences?
d) _ , _ , 36, 40, _ , 48, _
e) 16, 7, _ , −11, _ , _

(You will find a TIP to help you with NUMBER SEQUENCES on page 29)

TIPS FOR MATHS SUCCESS

PAGES 6–7

STUNT WORK FILE

Measuring time:
TIP: There are 60 minutes in one hour.

PAGES 8–9

CHALLENGE QUESTIONS

Finding the area of a shape:

TIP: To find the **area** of a shape you need to multiply the length and the width.

For example, this airbag would have an area of 50 square feet (50 ft^2).

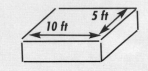

Multiplication:

Here are two of the ways you can set out multiplications:

The grid method

12 x 8

X	10	2	
8	80	16	= 96

Partitioning

14 x 12

	14
x	12
14 x 10	140
14 x 2	28
	168

Finding the volume of a shape:

A cubic foot looks like this:

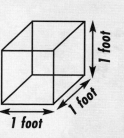

1ft x 1ft x 1ft = 1 cubic foot

TIP: One foot is about 30 centimetres.
(For more information on UNITS OF MEASUREMENT see page 29)

PAGES 10–11

STUNT WORK FILE

Measuring time:
TIP: There are 60 seconds in a minute.

PAGES 12–13

STUNT WORK FILE

Making turns and measuring angles:
Angle is a measure of turn. Angles are measured in **degrees**. The symbol for degrees is °.

One whole turn (a complete revolution) is 360°.

A quarter turn is 90° or one *right angle.*

There are four *right angles* in one whole turn.

The angles at the corners of squares and rectangles always measure 90˚.

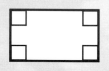

PAGES 14–15

STUNT WORK FILE

Calculations:
When finding missing numbers it helps to remember that for every number statement there are three related number facts. If we know 8 x 2 = 16, then we can also write:

2 x 8 = 16
16 ÷ 2 = 8
16 ÷ 8 = 2

So the missing number in any of these statements could be 2, 8 or 16 depending on the position of the missing number and whether the fact is a multiplication or division fact.

PAGES 16–17

CHALLENGE QUESTIONS

Place value:
Place value means that the *place* a digit has in a number, tells us its *value*.
For example, the '2' in 23 means 2 tens (20).
The '2' in 32 is 2 units. It is important to write numbers carefully, with each digit in the correct place.

PAGES 18–19

STUNT WORK FILE
Using co-ordinates:
The diagram of the stunt plan is actually a grid map.

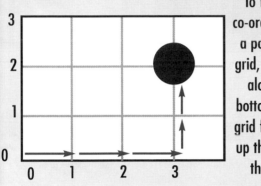

To find the co-ordinates of a point on a grid, you look along the bottom of the grid first, then up the side of the grid.

For example, a grid reference of **(3,2)** means **3 steps** along the bottom then **2 steps** up to find the exact point.

PAGES 20–21

STUNT WORK FILE
Handling data:

When you are comparing different sets of information, it can be useful to put them in a chart like this:

STUNTMAN	SKILLS		
	Car bail-out	Fire burn	Skydiving
ALEC	✔	✔	
PAUL	✔		✔
DAVID	✔	✔	
CHRIS			✔
ED	✔		✔

PAGES 22–23

STUNT WORK FILE

TIP: When adding up sums of money it is helpful to write them down underneath one another in a column. Remember to list them carefully, for example, hundreds under hundreds, tens under tens.

PAGES 24–25

STUNT WORK FILE
Estimating using a number line:
TIP: The camera track is a number line. A number line is continuous and extends forever in both directions. We can decide on the length of the line we need according to the numbers we are working with.

This line extends from 0.1 to 0.2, with some points in between marked:

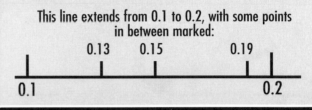

0.13   0.15   0.19

0.1   0.2

PAGES 26–27

CHALLENGE QUESTIONS
Extending number sequences:
TIP: When looking at number sequences, try working out the difference between pairs of numbers to find the pattern. For example, in the sequence 2, 6, 10, _, you can work out that the difference between *2 and 6*, and *6 and 10* is 4, so the next number in the sequence will be 14.

UNITS OF MEASUREMENT

We use two systems of measurement in the UK: *metric* (centimetres, metres, kilometres, grams, kilograms) and *imperial* (inches, feet, miles, ounces, pounds).

METRIC		IMPERIAL	
Length		**Length**	
1 millimetre (mm)		1 inch (in)	
1 centimetre (cm)	= 10 mm	1 foot (ft)	= 12 in
1 metre (m)	= 100 cm	1 yard (yd)	= 3 ft
1 kilometre (km)	= 1000 m	1 mile	= 1760 yd
Weight		**Weight**	
1 gram (g)		1 ounce (oz)	
1 kilogram (kg)	= 1000 g	1 pound (lb)	= 16 oz
Capacity		**Capacity**	
1 millilitre (ml)		1 fluid ounce (fl oz)	
1 litre (l)	= 1000 ml	1 UK pint (pt)	= 20 fl oz

Comparing metric and imperial measurements:

1 kilometre = 0.62 of a mile

1 kilogram = 2.2 pounds

0.57 litre = 1 UK pint

ANSWERS ANSWERS ANSWERS

PAGES 6–7

STUNT WORK FILE

1) 10:55 am – on **set** rehearsing a sword fight.
   6:35 am – on a two mile run.
   5:15 pm – on set filming a sword fight.
   7:47 pm – at sub-aqua training.
2) The stuntman spent 4 hours and 5 minutes rehearsing the sword fight.
3) The stuntman is on set after lunch for 5 hours and 15 minutes.
4) The meeting was 30 minutes long.

CHALLENGE QUESTIONS

a) In every 2 weeks, the stuntwoman spends 28 hours training.
b) In every 3 weeks, the stuntwoman spends 42 hours training.
c) In every 10 weeks, the stuntwoman spends 140 hours training.

PAGES 8–9

STUNT WORK FILE

1) G7 2) H5
3) E2, D2, E3, D3 – you can also place one in E4 to be extra careful.
4) D7, D6, E6, F6, G6, G7   5) D5, E5, E4, E3, D3

CHALLENGE QUESTIONS

a) 30 ft fall airbag: 96 square feet (96 ft^2)
   50 ft fall airbag: 168 square feet (168 ft^2)
   70 ft fall airbag: 210 square feet (210 ft^2)
   100 ft fall airbag: 500 square feet (500 ft^2)
   150 ft fall airbag: 750 square feet (750 ft^2)
b) 5000 cubic feet of air will be in the airbag.

PAGES 10–11

STUNT WORK FILE

1) 16.8 seconds   2) 3.5 seconds
3) 11:08 and 15 seconds

CHALLENGE QUESTIONS

c) S T U N T M A N

PAGES 12–13

STUNT WORK FILE

1) a) 45° b) 270° c) 90° d) 60°
2) The car has turned through 180° (a half turn).
3) The car has turned through 360° (one whole turn).

CHALLENGE QUESTIONS

a) The stopping distance is 39 metres.
b) The car is 4.5 metres long.
c) The car is travelling at 70 mph.

PAGES 14–15

STUNT WORK FILE

ROUTE 1	ROUTE 2	ROUTE 3
$40 \div 10 = 4$	$14 + 9 = 23$	$14 + 9 = 23$
$62 - 37 = 25$	$11 + 7 + 12 = 30$	$96 - 17 = 79$
$160 \div 5 = 32$	$62 - 37 = 25$	$24 \div 3 = 8$
$22 \div 2 = 11$	$160 \div 5 = 32$	$4 \times 3 = 12$
$5 \times 2 = 10$		
The sum of the missing numbers is 80	The sum of the missing numbers is 104	The sum of the missing numbers is 113

ROUTE 4	ROUTE 5
$95 - 32 = 63$	$95 - 32 = 63$
$11 + 7 + 12 = 30$	$49 - 38 = 11$
$24 \div 3 = 8$	$13 + 24 = 37$
$22 \div 2 = 11$	$96 - 17 = 79$
$72 \div 8 = 9$	$24 \div 3 = 8$
	$22 \div 2 = 11$
	$5 \times 2 = 10$
The sum of the missing numbers is 189	The sum of the missing numbers is 240

CHALLENGE QUESTIONS

a) Doug Danger's jumbo jet jump was 48.77 metres.
(The answer 48.768 has been rounded up.)
b) Jason Rennie's MONSTER ramp-to-ramp jump is the longest.

ANSWERS ANSWERS ANSWERS

PAGES 16–17

STUNT WORK FILE

1) 200 feet 2) 2000 feet 3) 13 500 feet

4) 67.5 seconds (1 minute and 7 ½ seconds.)

CHALLENGE QUESTIONS

a) Thousands b) Tens c) Hundreds

d) Tens of thousands

PAGES 18–19

STUNT WORK FILE

1) 5 whole squares   2) 11 whole squares

3) • The boat (7,10)   • Pulley wheel B (2, 10)

   • The truck (2,2)

4) Pulley wheel A is found at point (2,8).

5) The crash will happen at (5,10)

CHALLENGE QUESTIONS

a) The car is south-east of pulley B.

b) The truck is south-west of pulley C.

PAGES 20–21

STUNT WORK FILE

1) Paul 2) Paul 3) Alec, David and Ed 4) David

  5) The TV commercial: Ed

      The hospital drama: Paul

      The "Countdown" movie: Alec and David

CHALLENGE QUESTION

Alec wearing a brown wig, or with his hair dyed brown, would be the best stunt double for the "Countdown" actor.

PAGES 22–23

STUNT WORK FILE

1) £3000 2) £3200 3) £8000 4) £500 5) £36 100

CHALLENGE QUESTIONS

The following measurements are closest to actual happenings:

  a) 50 mph b) ¼ second c) 50 cm

PAGES 24–25

STUNT WORK FILE

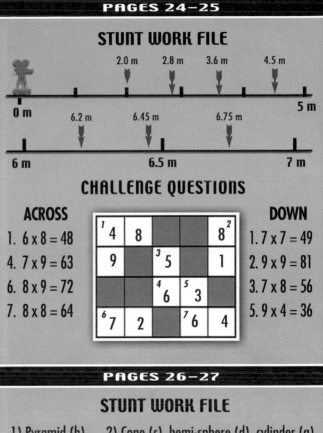

CHALLENGE QUESTIONS

ACROSS

1. 6 x 8 = 48

4. 7 x 9 = 63

6. 8 x 9 = 72

7. 8 x 8 = 64

DOWN

1. 7 x 7 = 49

2. 9 x 9 = 81

3. 7 x 8 = 56

5. 9 x 4 = 36

PAGES 26–27

STUNT WORK FILE

1) Pyramid (h)   2) Cone (c), hemi-sphere (d), cylinder (g)

3) Pentagonal **prism** (a), hexagonal prism (b), rectangular prism or cuboid (e), triangular prism (f)

4) Pentagonal prism 15 **edges**, hexagonal prism 18 edges, rectangular prism or cuboid 12 edges, triangular prism 9 edges

5) The number of the straight edges in a prism is a product in the three times table (a multiple of three).

CHALLENGE QUESTIONS

a) 40, 47, 54   b) 113, 116, 119

c) 20, 17, 14   d) 28, 32, _ , _ , 44, _ , 52

e) _ , _ , –2, _ , –20, –29

GLOSSARY

BUDGET The amount of money that can be spent on a film or part of a film, such as a stunt.

DOLLY A special type of trolley with four wheels. Dollies are used for moving cameras around during filming.

EDITED When all the separate sections of film are put together at the end of filming.

FREEFALLING When skydivers are falling towards the earth at a great speed, before their parachutes are open.

GRIP A film or TV technician who rigs (sets up) the cameras, and moves them around during filming.

LANDING RIG An airbag, crash mats or a pile of cardboard boxes, set up for a stuntman or stuntwoman to land on.

PLOTS The stories in movies.

PYROTECHNICIAN A special effects person who is an expert at setting up explosions and fires.

SCRIPT The text of a play, film or TV programme. The script includes all the actors' lines (words) and instructions for their actions.

SET The setting for a film, TV programme or play. Sets are created inside a studio using scenery. Sometimes real buildings or places are used as a set.

SHOOTING Another word for filming.

SHOT The basic building blocks of a movie or TV programme. A shot is an uninterrupted run of the camera during filming. In the finished movie or TV programme, lots of shots are joined together through editing.

SPECIAL EFFECTS The area of movie-making involved in setting up dramatic effects, such as explosions. Special effects people also create monsters, make earthquakes happen, help actors to look as if they are flying and produce all the fantastic effects we love to see in movies and TV programmes. Special effects people use make-up, models, computer generated imagery and lots of clever tricks to make strange happenings look completely real.

MATHS GLOSSARY

3-D (THREE DIMENSIONAL) Shapes that have length (or height), width and depth (thickness).

ANGLE A measure of turn.

APEX The highest point of a flat (plane) shape or a 3-D shape.

AREA The measure of the size of a surface, made in squares (all of the same size).

CLOCKWISE To make a turn in the direction that the hands of a clock move. Anti-clockwise is to move in the opposite direction.

DEGREES The units used for measuring angles and temperatures.

EDGE The line where two faces of a solid shape meet.

ESTIMATE To find a number or amount that is close to an exact answer.

FACE A flat surface of a solid shape.

LINES OF SYMMETRY Lines that divide a shape into two matching halves.

PRISMS Solid shapes the same size and shape all along their length. If you slice through a prism parallel to its end face, the cut faces will be the same size and shape as the ends. All the faces of a prism are flat (plane) and have three or more sides.

t=top, b=bottom, c=centre, l=left, r=right, OFC=outside front cover, OBC=outside back cover

Alamy: OFC, 7tr, 7br, 21cr, 22-23c, 23b, 26-27c, OBCtl. Bickers Action: 15bl, 25tr. Corbis: 15. Joe Jennings (Skydive.tv): 1, 16-17, OBCcr. Stewart Johnson: 19. Peter Hassall: 8-9, 21c. Steve Truglia (prostunts.net): 6-7main, 10-11, 13, 20.

Every effort has been made to trace the copyright holders, and we apologize in advance for any unintentional omissions. We would be pleased to insert the appropriate acknowledgements in any subsequent edition of this publication.